25 Prophets of Islam

Bold indicates Arch-Prophets

Adam

Allah created the very first human, Adam, from sounding clay molded from black mud. Adam was no ordinary creation; Allah gave him a special honor and made him the first prophet. Allah taught Adam the names of everything around him—trees, animals, stars, and more. This gift of knowledge made Adam unique, showing that humans have the amazing ability to learn and understand. To celebrate Adam's creation, Allah commanded the angels to bow to him as a sign of respect. Everyone obeyed, except Iblis, who refused out of jealousy and pride.

Adam lived in a beautiful garden with his wife, Hawwa. They were happy there, but Allah gave them one important rule: not to eat from a certain tree. Iblis, still angry and jealous, tricked them into breaking that rule. When Adam and Hawwa realized their mistake, they felt very sorry and asked Allah for forgiveness. Allah, who is always kind and merciful, forgave them. But as part of their new journey, Allah sent them to live on Earth, where they would start the family of humanity.

Adam's story teaches us some very important lessons. It reminds us that everyone makes mistakes, but what matters most is being sorry and trying to do better. It also shows us how special humans are, with the ability to learn, love, and take care of the world. Adam was the beginning of our big human family and a reminder that Allah's mercy is always there for us.

1

Idris

After Adam, Allah chose another special prophet, Idris, to guide the people. Idris was a wise and kind man, known for his deep love of learning. Allah blessed Idris with great knowledge and skills, and he taught people how to write, measure, and even sew clothes. Before Idris, people didn't know how to stitch fabric together, but he showed them how to use a needle and thread. He also encouraged everyone to be honest, work hard, and remember Allah in everything they did.

Idris loved spending time in worship and prayer. He was so close to Allah that he would often climb to the tops of mountains or sit under the stars, speaking to Allah with a heart full of devotion. The people admired his wisdom and followed his teachings, learning how to live peacefully and help one another. Idris reminded them that doing good deeds and staying true to Allah's path would bring them happiness in this life and the next.

Because of his pure heart and unshakable faith, Allah honored Idris in a very special way. The Quran tells us that Allah raised Idris to a high place, showing just how beloved he was. His story teaches us that seeking knowledge, working hard, and staying close to Allah are ways to live a life filled with purpose and blessings.

3

Nuh

A long time after Idris, there lived a prophet named Nuh. Allah chose Nuh to guide his people because they had forgotten how to worship Allah and were doing many wrong things. Nuh loved his people and wanted to help them, so he taught them about Allah, reminded them to be kind to one another, and told them to stop worshipping idols. He spoke to them with gentleness and patience, hoping they would change their ways.

But many people refused to listen. They made fun of Nuh and ignored his message. Year after year, Nuh kept trying, never giving up because he cared so much for his people. Finally, Allah told Nuh that it was time to prepare for a great flood that would wash away all the wrongdoing. Allah instructed Nuh to build a massive ark, and Nuh began working, following Allah's guidance. People laughed at him even more, but Nuh trusted Allah completely.

When the rain began to fall and the waters rose, Nuh gathered his family, the believers, and pairs of animals into the ark. The flood covered the Earth, but everyone on the ark was safe because they had listened to Allah. When the flood ended, Nuh and his followers stepped onto dry land, grateful to Allah for saving them. Nuh's story teaches us the importance of patience, trust in Allah, and standing firm in doing what is right, even when it's difficult.

5

Hud

A long time ago, there was a powerful and wealthy people called the people of 'Ad. They lived in a land with tall buildings and strong fortresses, surrounded by beautiful gardens and fields. But instead of thanking Allah for their blessings, the people of 'Ad became arrogant. They started worshipping idols and behaving unkindly. Allah, in His mercy, sent Prophet Hud to guide them back to the right path.

Hud was a wise and brave man who loved his people dearly. He told them, "My people, worship Allah alone. He is the one who gave you all these blessings. Stop worshipping idols and turn to Allah with thankfulness." But most of them didn't listen. They laughed at Hud and said, "Who are you to tell us what to do? We are strong and don't need anyone's help." Despite their arrogance, Hud remained patient and kept warning them about Allah's punishment if they didn't change their ways.

Sadly, the people of 'Ad refused to listen. Then, just as Hud had warned, Allah sent a mighty windstorm that blew for days and nights, destroying everything in its path. Only Hud and the believers who followed him were saved. Hud's story teaches us that true strength comes from humbling ourselves before Allah and being kind and grateful, no matter how powerful or rich we might be.

Saleh

After the people of 'Ad, there came another group of people called the Thamud. They were skilled builders and lived in magnificent homes carved into mountains. Allah had blessed them with wealth and strength, but instead of being grateful, they worshipped idols and became proud and unjust. To guide them, Allah sent Prophet Saleh, a kind and gentle man who loved his people deeply.

Saleh told them, "My people, worship Allah alone. He is the one who gave you everything you enjoy. Be grateful and stop doing wrong." Some people believed him and started following Allah's path, but most of them laughed and said, "Saleh, prove to us that your message is true." They demanded a miracle to show Allah's power. Allah granted their request, and from the rocky mountains, a great she-camel appeared, just as they had asked.

Saleh told them, "This camel is a sign from Allah. Let her drink from the well freely, and don't harm her." But the disbelievers were stubborn and cruel. They hurt the camel and refused to listen to Saleh's warnings. Then Allah's punishment came upon them—a mighty earthquake shook their land, leaving only Saleh and the believers safe. Saleh's story reminds us to respect Allah's blessings, be kind, and always follow the truth, no matter what others say.

9

Ibrahim

A long time ago, there lived a man named Ibrahim, known for his wisdom and strong faith in Allah. Ibrahim grew up in a land where people worshipped idols—statues made of stone and wood. Even as a young boy, Ibrahim knew these idols could not hear, see, or help anyone. He often wondered, "How can these lifeless things be our gods?" Ibrahim wanted his people to understand the truth, so he began to ask them questions and gently guide them toward worshipping Allah alone.

One day, Ibrahim came up with a bold plan to show his people that their idols were powerless. While everyone was away, he went to the temple and destroyed all the idols except for the biggest one. When the people returned and saw what had happened, they were shocked. "Who did this to our gods?" they asked. Ibrahim told them to ask the largest idol, knowing it couldn't answer. The people realized their idols had no power, but instead of changing their ways, they became angry and tried to harm Ibrahim. Allah protected him from their plans, showing that Ibrahim's faith was stronger than their anger.

Ibrahim's trust in Allah was tested many times, but he always obeyed with a faithful heart. When Allah commanded him to leave his homeland or sacrifice something dear to him, Ibrahim never hesitated. Because of his unwavering trust, Allah blessed Ibrahim with two sons, Ismail and Ishaq, who would also become prophets. Ibrahim's story teaches us the importance of faith, courage, and trusting Allah, even when the path seems difficult. Through his life, we learn that true strength comes from believing in and obeying Allah alone.

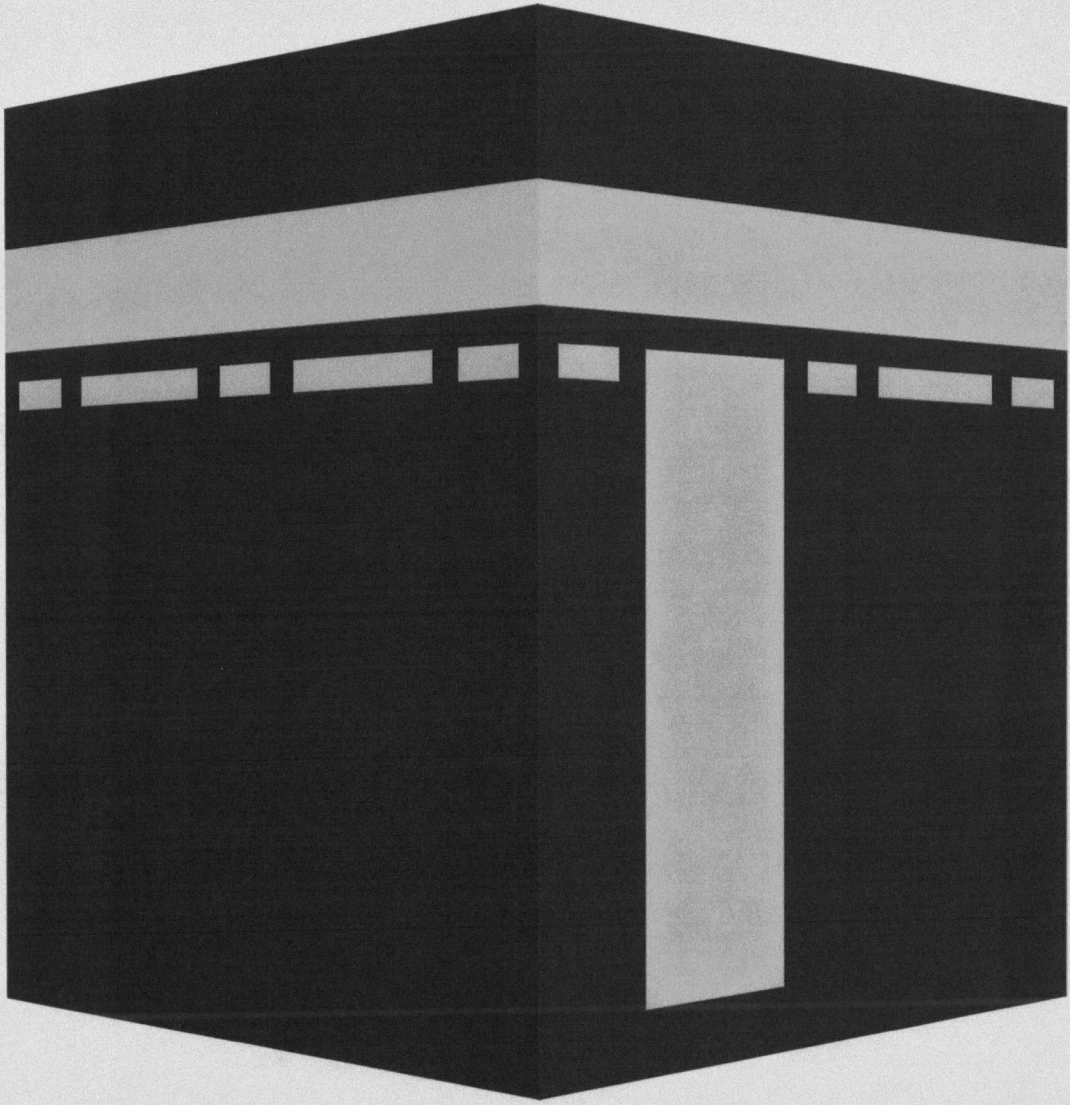

Lut

During the time of Prophet Ibrahim, there lived a man named Lut, who was also chosen by Allah to guide the people. Lut was sent to a city where the people had fallen into terrible behavior. They committed acts of injustice, treated one another cruelly, and turned away from Allah. Prophet Lut cared deeply for them and wanted to help them live better, kinder lives.

Lut spoke to the people with patience and love, saying, "My people, turn to Allah and stop the wrong things you are doing. Be fair and kind to one another, and remember that Allah sees everything." But most of the people didn't want to listen. Instead, they mocked Lut and ignored his warnings. Despite this, Lut never gave up, continuing to invite them to do what was right and pleasing to Allah.

Finally, Allah sent His angels to Lut with a message: the city would face a severe punishment because of its wickedness. Lut and the few believers were told to leave the city at night and not look back. When the punishment came, it was swift and just, and the city was destroyed. Lut and the believers were safe because they trusted Allah and followed His guidance. The story of Lut teaches us to stand firm in what is right, stay away from wrongdoing, and trust that Allah always rewards those who remain faithful to Him.

13

Ismail

Ismail was the beloved son of Prophet Ibrahim and a great prophet himself. His story begins with a remarkable event. Allah commanded Ibrahim to take his wife, Hajar, and their baby son, Ismail, to a desert valley where no one lived. It was a barren place with no food or water, but Ibrahim trusted Allah's plan. After leaving them there, Ibrahim prayed, "O Allah, take care of my family and make this land a place of blessings."

Hajar, a strong and faithful woman, cared for little Ismail. When their water ran out, she ran back and forth between two hills, Safa and Marwah, searching for help. Suddenly, Allah sent the angel Jibril, who caused water to gush from the ground at Ismail's feet. This spring, known as Zamzam, became a source of life in the desert and remains a blessing for people to this day. The valley grew into the holy city of Makkah, where Ismail and his family lived.

As Ismail grew older, Allah tested both him and Ibrahim with a great command. Ibrahim dreamed that Allah wanted him to sacrifice Ismail. When he told Ismail about this, Ismail, full of faith, said, "Father, do as Allah has commanded. You will find me patient." Just as Ibrahim was about to carry out the sacrifice, Allah stopped him and replaced Ismail with a ram, showing that it was a test of their faith. Ismail's story teaches us about obedience, trust in Allah, and the power of faith, no matter how challenging the test may seem.

Ishaq

Ishaq, the son of Prophet Ibrahim, was a blessing given to Ibrahim and his wife Sarah in their old age. For many years, they had prayed for a child, and Allah answered their prayers with the promise of a son. Ishaq was not just a gift of love for his parents but also chosen by Allah to be a prophet, continuing the noble mission of his father, Ibrahim.

Ishaq grew up in a family devoted to Allah and surrounded by wisdom and faith. Ibrahim taught him the importance of worshipping Allah alone and living a life filled with kindness and gratitude. As Ishaq grew older, he became a wise and gentle man, guiding the people to follow Allah's path. He reminded them to worship Allah, be just, and treat one another with fairness and compassion.

Allah blessed Ishaq with many descendants, including other prophets, making him part of a special lineage that spread Allah's message far and wide. Ishaq's life is a story of blessings and the fulfillment of Allah's promises. It teaches us that patience and trust in Allah's plans bring great rewards and that families rooted in faith can shine as a source of goodness and guidance for others.

17

Ya'qub

Ya'qub, also known as Jacob, was the son of Prophet Ishaq and the grandson of Prophet Ibrahim. He was a man of great faith and wisdom, chosen by Allah to continue spreading His message. Ya'qub had twelve sons, and his family was known for their deep connection to Allah. Because of this, Ya'qub was also called "Israel," and his descendants became known as the Children of Israel.

Ya'qub was a loving father who taught his children to worship Allah and live with kindness and honesty. Among his sons was Yusuf, who was especially close to Ya'qub's heart. This special bond made some of his other sons jealous, and they did something very hurtful by taking Yusuf away and pretending he was gone forever. Even though Ya'qub was heartbroken, he never lost hope in Allah. He kept praying and trusting that Allah would one day reunite him with Yusuf.

Allah blessed Ya'qub for his patience and unshakable faith. Many years later, he was joyfully reunited with Yusuf, who had grown up to be a great leader. Ya'qub's story teaches us about the power of patience, the importance of trusting Allah during difficult times, and the value of family and forgiveness. His life reminds us that Allah's plans are always full of wisdom, even when we can't see them right away.

19

Yusuf

Yusuf, the son of Ya'qub, was a boy of extraordinary beauty and a pure heart. One night, he had a dream where the sun, the moon, and eleven stars bowed down to him. When he told his father, Prophet Ya'qub, about the dream, his father understood it was a special sign from Allah and told Yusuf to keep it a secret. But Yusuf's brothers were jealous of how much their father loved him, and they decided to do something cruel—they threw him into a deep well and left him there alone.

A group of travelers passing by the well found Yusuf and took him to Egypt, where he was sold as a servant. Despite these hardships, Yusuf never stopped trusting Allah. Over time, his honesty, kindness, and wisdom earned him respect. Even when he was wrongfully imprisoned, Yusuf's faith in Allah remained strong. In prison, Allah gave him the gift of interpreting dreams, which later led to his freedom when he correctly explained the king's troubling dream about a famine.

Yusuf eventually became a trusted leader in Egypt, helping the country prepare for the famine. In a beautiful twist, his brothers, who didn't recognize him, came to Egypt seeking food during the famine. Yusuf forgave them for their past wrongs and revealed his identity, reuniting with his family in a moment of pure joy. Yusuf's story teaches us about the power of patience, forgiveness, and trusting Allah's plan, no matter how difficult life may seem. His life is a shining example of how faith and kindness lead to great rewards.

21

Ayub

Ayub, also known as Job, was a prophet blessed by Allah with great wealth, a loving family, and good health. He was known for his kindness, generosity, and constant devotion to Allah. Ayub would always thank Allah for his blessings, no matter how small or big they were. But Ayub's faith was about to be tested in a way few could imagine.

One day, Ayub lost everything—his wealth, his children, and even his health. He became very ill, and his body grew weak. Despite all this, Ayub never complained. He remained patient and kept praising Allah, saying, "Allah has given me so much in the past, and if He takes it away, I will still be grateful." Even when people turned away from him, his heart stayed full of love and trust in Allah.

After many years of patience and unwavering faith, Allah rewarded Ayub for his steadfastness. He healed Ayub, restored his health, gave him even more wealth, and blessed him with a beautiful family once again. Ayub's story teaches us that no matter how difficult life gets, patience and trust in Allah will lead to better days. It reminds us that true strength lies in staying grateful and faithful, even during life's hardest trials.

23

Shu'aib

Shu'aib was a wise and gentle prophet sent to guide the people of Madyan. The people of Madyan lived in a beautiful land, but instead of being grateful, they turned away from Allah. They cheated others by giving less in trade, were dishonest in their dealings, and treated one another unfairly. Allah, in His mercy, sent Shu'aib to help them change their ways.

Shu'aib spoke to his people with kindness, saying, "My people, worship Allah alone. Be fair and honest in your trade, and do not cheat others. Remember, Allah sees everything you do." While a few people listened to Shu'aib and believed in his message, most of them mocked him and refused to change. They said, "Why should we follow you? We will live as we please!" Shu'aib warned them that their actions would bring Allah's punishment, but they didn't listen.

Finally, Allah's punishment came upon the disbelievers—a terrible earthquake that destroyed their city. Only Shu'aib and the believers who followed him were saved. Shu'aib's story teaches us the importance of honesty, fairness, and treating others with kindness. It reminds us that greed and dishonesty only lead to loss, while living a life of truth and gratitude brings blessings and peace.

Musa

A long time ago, in the land of Egypt, a baby boy named Musa was born. At that time, the Pharaoh, a cruel and powerful king, feared that the children of the Israelites would grow up and challenge his rule. To stop this, he ordered all the baby boys to be taken away. But Allah had a special plan for Musa. His mother, trusting Allah, placed him in a basket and let it float down the river. The basket was found by the Pharaoh's wife, who loved the baby and decided to raise him in the palace as her own.

Musa grew up in the palace but always felt connected to the Israelites, his true people. One day, while defending an oppressed man, Musa accidentally hurt someone and fled Egypt in fear. In a distant land, he started a new life, working as a shepherd and starting a family. It was during this time that Allah called Musa to be a prophet. At the foot of Mount Sinai, Allah spoke to Musa and gave him a mission: to return to Egypt and free the Israelites from Pharaoh's oppression.

With Allah's help, Musa performed amazing miracles, like turning his staff into a snake and parting the Red Sea. These signs showed Pharaoh and his people Allah's power, but Pharaoh refused to believe. Finally, Musa led the Israelites out of Egypt and to safety. Along the way, Allah gave Musa the Torah, a guide for his people. Musa's story teaches us about courage, trusting Allah, and standing up for what is right, even when the odds seem impossible. His life is a powerful reminder that Allah is always with those who believe in Him.

27

Harun

Harun, also known as Aaron, was the brother of Prophet Musa and a prophet chosen by Allah to help guide the Israelites. When Allah commanded Musa to confront the Pharaoh and free the Israelites, Musa felt nervous about speaking to such a powerful and cruel king. So, he asked Allah for help, and Allah made Harun his companion in this mission. Harun was gifted with a gentle way of speaking, which made him an excellent helper and support for Musa.

Together, Musa and Harun stood before Pharaoh, delivering Allah's message. They told him to stop oppressing the Israelites and to believe in Allah. Harun spoke with kindness and patience, but Pharaoh refused to listen. Even when Allah sent signs, like turning Musa's staff into a snake and bringing plagues to Egypt, Pharaoh and his people remained stubborn. Harun continued to stand by Musa, helping him guide the Israelites toward freedom.

Harun's role didn't end there. After Musa led the Israelites out of Egypt, Harun helped guide the people in their new life. He reminded them to stay faithful to Allah and follow His commands. Harun's story teaches us the importance of teamwork, supporting one another in doing good, and staying patient and kind even in difficult times. His life reminds us that we are stronger when we work together for a shared purpose, especially in serving Allah.

29

Dhul-Kifl

Dhul-Kifl was a prophet known for his steadfastness, fairness, and devotion to Allah. Although the Quran does not detail his story, scholars believe he was a man of great patience and wisdom, chosen by Allah to guide his people. His name, "Dhul-Kifl," means "the man of responsibility," and he earned this title because of his ability to handle challenges with grace and justice.

Dhul-Kifl's life was marked by his commitment to doing good and helping others. He treated everyone with fairness and kindness, ensuring that justice was upheld in his community. Even when life became difficult, Dhul-Kifl remained patient, never giving up on his duties or his trust in Allah. He inspired others to stay strong in their faith and to always strive for what was right.

The story of Dhul-Kifl reminds us that being responsible, kind, and patient are qualities that please Allah. His example teaches us to fulfill our promises, help those in need, and remain faithful no matter what challenges we face. Though his life may seem simple, it holds a powerful lesson: even in the smallest acts of goodness, there is great reward from Allah.

31

Dawud

Dawud, also known as David, was a prophet chosen by Allah for his wisdom, courage, and strong faith. As a young man, Dawud became famous for his bravery when he faced a mighty warrior named Goliath (Jalut). With nothing but a sling and his trust in Allah, Dawud defeated Goliath, showing that true strength comes from faith, not size or weapons. This victory made him a hero among his people and marked the beginning of his remarkable journey.

Allah blessed Dawud in many ways. He made him a king and a prophet, giving him the responsibility to lead his people with justice and fairness. Dawud was known for his deep sense of fairness; he always listened carefully to disputes and judged wisely. Allah also gave him a beautiful voice, and Dawud would sing praises to Allah, filling the mountains and birds with joy as they joined in harmony.

One of Dawud's greatest achievements was receiving the Zabur, a holy book revealed by Allah. The Zabur was filled with wisdom and guidance, teaching people how to live righteously. Dawud's story reminds us that faith, courage, and fairness are qualities that can lead to great success. It also teaches us the importance of being grateful for Allah's blessings and using them to help others and spread goodness in the world.

33

Sulayman

Suleyman, also known as Solomon, was a prophet and king, blessed by Allah with great wisdom, knowledge, and a unique ability to understand and communicate with animals and even the jinn. From a young age, Suleyman showed remarkable intelligence and fairness. When disputes arose, people often came to him for guidance, and his wise judgments earned him respect from all.

As a king, Suleyman ruled a vast and powerful kingdom with kindness and justice. Allah gave him extraordinary gifts, such as commanding the wind and controlling the jinn to build magnificent structures. One of the most famous stories about Suleyman is when he listened to the concerns of an ant. While leading his army, he heard the ants warning each other to stay out of the way. Suleyman smiled, understanding their language, and thanked Allah for giving him such incredible abilities.

Suleyman's kingdom was a shining example of how faith and wisdom can bring peace and harmony. Despite all his power, he remained humble and always remembered that his blessings were from Allah. His life teaches us that true greatness comes from gratitude, kindness, and using our abilities to help others. Suleyman's story inspires us to be just, compassionate, and always mindful of Allah's blessings.

35

Ilyas

Ilyas, also known as Elijah, was a prophet sent by Allah to guide the people of a land that had turned away from worshipping Allah. The people had begun worshipping a false god named Baal and had forgotten the teachings of the prophets who came before Ilyas. They lived selfishly and disobeyed Allah, turning to idols instead of seeking the truth. Ilyas, with his pure heart and strong faith, was sent to remind them of the One True God.

With patience and courage, Ilyas spoke to his people, saying, "Why do you worship a false god that cannot hear or help you? Allah is the Creator of the heavens and the earth. Worship Him alone, and you will find peace." But most of the people ignored Ilyas, mocked him, and continued their ways. Only a few believed in his message and stayed loyal to Allah.

When the people refused to change, Allah stopped sending rain, and the land suffered from drought and famine. Still, Ilyas remained steadfast, praying to Allah and continuing his mission. In the end, Ilyas was taken by Allah to a special place, honored for his dedication and unwavering faith. His story teaches us to always stay true to Allah, no matter how difficult life becomes, and to trust that Allah rewards those who remain faithful and steadfast in spreading the truth.

Alyasa

Alyasa, also known as Elisha, was a prophet chosen by Allah to continue the mission of Prophet Ilyas. After Ilyas was taken by Allah, Alyasa took on the responsibility of guiding the people. He lived among a community that had turned away from Allah and needed constant reminders to worship Him alone and to live with kindness and justice.

Alyasa was known for his patience and dedication. He tirelessly encouraged the people to turn back to Allah and abandon their wrong ways. Despite the challenges he faced, Alyasa remained firm in his faith and never gave up on his mission. Allah blessed him with wisdom and the ability to perform miracles, which helped him inspire those who believed and brought hope to his followers.

Though not much is detailed about Alyasa's life in the Quran, his story is a reminder of the importance of perseverance in doing what is right. He teaches us that even in difficult times, staying loyal to Allah and fulfilling our responsibilities can make a big difference. Alyasa's life encourages us to lead with patience, kindness, and unwavering trust in Allah's guidance.

39

Yunus

Yunus, also known as Jonah, was a prophet sent by Allah to guide the people of a city who had turned away from Him. The people were living in disobedience, worshipping idols and ignoring Allah's commands. Yunus tried to teach them about Allah and urged them to change their ways, but they refused to listen. Frustrated, Yunus left the city without waiting for Allah's permission, thinking the people would never change.

After leaving, Yunus boarded a ship, but during the journey, a great storm arose. The people on the ship believed someone had angered Allah, so they cast lots to decide who would leave the ship to calm the storm. The lot fell on Yunus. Knowing he had left his mission without Allah's command, Yunus jumped into the sea, where he was swallowed by a huge fish. Inside the belly of the fish, in complete darkness, Yunus realized his mistake. He prayed to Allah, saying, "There is no god but You. Glory be to You. Indeed, I was among the wrongdoers."

Allah, in His infinite mercy, forgave Yunus and caused the fish to release him onto the shore. Yunus returned to his mission, and to his surprise, the people of his city had repented and turned back to Allah. They welcomed Yunus and embraced his message. Yunus's story teaches us the importance of patience, trusting Allah's plan, and seeking forgiveness when we make mistakes. It reminds us that Allah is always merciful to those who sincerely turn to Him.

41

Zakariyya

Zakariyya, also known as Zechariah, was a kind and pious prophet chosen by Allah. He was devoted to teaching his people about Allah's guidance and spent his days worshipping and caring for the holy temple. Zakariyya was known for his gentle heart and strong faith, but there was one thing he longed for—he and his wife were unable to have children, and he deeply wished for a child to continue spreading Allah's message after him.

Even though Zakariyya and his wife were very old, he never lost hope in Allah's mercy. One day, while praying in the temple, he made a heartfelt dua: "My Lord, grant me from Yourself a good offspring. Indeed, You are the Hearer of prayers." Allah, in His boundless generosity, accepted Zakariyya's prayer. The angels brought him good news: he would have a son named Yahya (John), a child of great virtue and wisdom. Zakariyya was amazed and asked how this could happen given his old age, and Allah reminded him that He has the power to do all things.

When Yahya was born, Zakariyya raised him to be a righteous and obedient servant of Allah. Zakariyya's story teaches us the power of sincere prayer and trusting Allah's timing. It reminds us that no matter how impossible something may seem, Allah's mercy and ability know no limits. His life encourages us to stay patient, grateful, and full of hope in Allah's blessings.

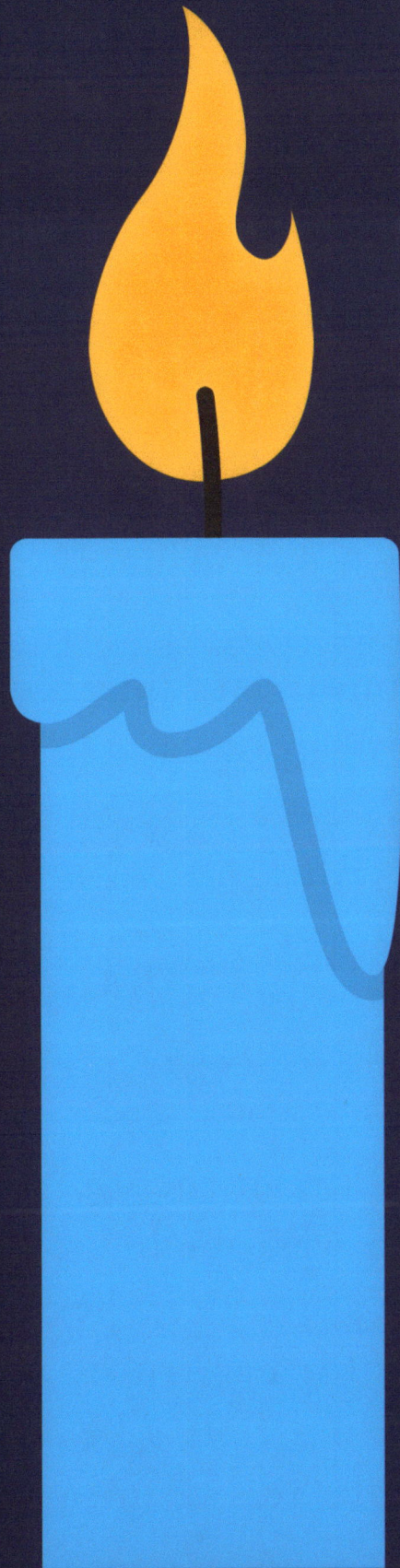

43

Yahya

Yahya, also known as John the Baptist, was the beloved son of Prophet Zakariya and a prophet chosen by Allah. From the moment he was born, Yahya was special. Allah gave him wisdom, kindness, and a pure heart, even as a young child. Yahya was known for his love of learning and his devotion to Allah. He grew up teaching others about Allah's guidance, spreading the message of truth and righteousness.

Yahya lived a simple and humble life, always staying close to Allah. He was known for his gentle and compassionate nature, always helping those in need. One of Yahya's greatest qualities was his courage—he stood up for what was right, even when it was difficult. He reminded people to worship Allah alone and to live lives of honesty and kindness.

Allah praised Yahya in the Quran, calling him a righteous servant who was obedient, pure, and respectful to his parents. Yahya's story teaches us to live with integrity, to stand up for the truth, and to always stay connected to Allah. His life is a beautiful example of how a kind and humble heart can inspire others and bring them closer to Allah.

45

Isa

Isa, also known as Jesus, was a prophet sent by Allah to guide the Children of Israel. His birth was a miraculous event, as he was born to Maryam (Mary) without a father. When the angel Jibril came to Maryam and told her she would have a child, she was amazed and asked, "How can I have a son when no man has touched me?" The angel replied that it was Allah's will, for He can do all things. Isa's miraculous birth was a sign of Allah's power and mercy.

From a young age, Isa showed signs of being chosen by Allah. He spoke as a baby to defend his mother's honor, saying, "I am a servant of Allah. He has given me the Scripture and made me a prophet." As he grew, Allah blessed Isa with wisdom and the ability to perform miracles. He healed the sick, gave sight to the blind, and even brought the dead back to life—all by Allah's permission. Isa always reminded people that these miracles were signs from Allah and that they should worship Him alone.

Isa faced many challenges, as some people rejected his message and plotted against him. But Allah protected Isa and raised him to the heavens. Muslims believe that Isa will return one day to complete his mission. His story is a powerful reminder of Allah's mercy, the importance of faith, and the strength to stand for the truth. Isa's life teaches us to stay humble, help others, and always trust in Allah's plan.

47

Muhammed

Muhammad, peace and blessings be upon him, was the final prophet sent by Allah to guide all of humanity. Born in the city of Makkah, he grew up as an orphan but was known for his honesty, kindness, and fairness. People trusted him so much that they called him Al-Amin, the trustworthy. As he grew older, Muhammad often spent time in quiet reflection, thinking about the Creator and the problems in his community, where people worshipped idols and treated one another unfairly.

One night, while meditating in the Cave of Hira, the angel Jibril appeared to him with a message from Allah. Jibril said, "Read!" Even though Muhammad couldn't read, he responded with courage and listened carefully as the first verses of the Quran were revealed to him. This marked the beginning of his mission as a prophet. Allah commanded Muhammad to teach people to worship Him alone, live justly, and care for one another. Despite facing many hardships, Muhammad remained patient and determined, spreading Allah's message with love and wisdom.

Over time, more and more people followed his teachings, and Muhammad's life became an example of mercy, honesty, and humility. He taught people to be kind to the poor, fair in their dealings, and forgiving toward others. As the final prophet, Muhammad completed Allah's guidance for humanity through the Quran and his example, known as the Sunnah. His story teaches us how to live a life of goodness, compassion, and faith. Muhammad's life inspires us to always strive for what is right and to trust Allah in all things.

www.ingramcontent.com/pod-product-compliance
Lightning Source LLC
Chambersburg PA
CBHW042022080426
42735CB00003B/134